Overview *Making a Boo[k]*

A children's book author explains ho[w ...] are made.

Reading Vocabulary Words

publish
brainstorm
editor

High-Frequency Words

ideas
way
come
write

cows
book
with
take

Building Future Vocabulary

* These vocabulary words do not appear in this text. They are provided to develop related oral vocabulary that first appears in future texts.

Words:	shelf	address	pointed
Levels:	Purple	Silver	Turquoise

Comprehension Strategy

Asking questions to understand the author

Fluency Skill

Taking a breath at appropriate times

Phonics Skill

Developing and applying knowledge of consonant digraphs: *ch* (<u>ch</u>ildren, <u>ch</u>ecks) and *ph* (<u>ph</u>otogra<u>ph</u>s, <u>ph</u>otogra<u>ph</u>er)

Reading-Writing Connection

Writing a book

[...] Colors Take-Home Books for children to share with their families.

Differentiated Instruction

Before reading the text, query children to discover their level of understanding of the comprehension strategy — Asking questions to understand the author. As you work together, provide additional support to children who show a beginning mastery of the strategy.

Focus on ELL

- Show a children's book. Point to and name its features, including text, cover, and artwork.

- Give children a different book and have them name its features.

T1

Using This Teaching Version

1 Before Reading

1. Before Reading

2. During Reading

3. Revisiting the Text

4. Assessment

This Teaching Version will assist you in directing children through the process of reading.

1. **Begin with Before Reading** to familiarize children with the book's content. Select the skills and strategies that meet the needs of your children.

2. **Next, go to During Reading** to help children become familiar with the text, and then to read individually on their own.

3. **Then, go back to Revisiting the Text** and select those specific activities that meet children's needs.

4. **Finally, finish with Assessment** to confirm children are ready to move forward to the next text.

Building Background

- Write *brainstorm* on the board. Read it aloud. Tell children this is a compound word. Ask them what two words they see. (*brain* and *storm*) Discuss how coming up with ideas is like a storm, or flurry of activity, in the brain.

- Introduce the book by reading the title, talking about the cover photograph, and sharing the overview.

Building Future Vocabulary
Use Interactive Modeling Card: Word Log

- Write the words *shelf, address,* and *pointed* in the first column of the Word Log.

- Have children look up each word in a dictionary. Record definitions on the Word Log and encourage children to think about how each word is associated with *Making a Book*.

Introduction to Reading Vocabulary

- On blank cards write: *publish, brainstorm,* and *editor*. Read them aloud. Tell children these words will appear in the text of *Making a Book*.

- Use each word in a sentence for understanding.

Introduction to Comprehension Strategy

- Explain that asking questions helps readers understand what an author has written.
- Tell children they will be asking questions to understand more about the author of *Making a Book*. Explain that while they will not actually talk to the author, these questions will allow them to think about the author's writing.
- Show children the cover photograph. Explain that the woman pictured is the author of this book.

Introduction to Phonics

- List on the board: **chapter**, **children**, **checks**, **phone**, **photographs**, and **photographer**. Read the words aloud and point out that each word begins with two consonants, either *ch* or *ph*.
- With children, say the sounds that *ch* and *ph* make at the beginning of a word. Point out that the letters *ph* make the same sound as *f*.
- Read the title page text. Have children identify the word that begins with *ch*. (**chapter**)
- Have children look for other *ch* and *ph* words as they read *Making a Book*.

Modeling Fluency

- Read aloud page 4, modeling taking a breath at appropriate times.
- Talk about how fluent readers take a breath when they see a comma or when they see a period at the end of a sentence.

2 During Reading

Book Talk

Beginning on page T4, use the During Reading notes on the left-hand side to engage children in a book talk. On page 24, follow with Individual Reading.

During Reading

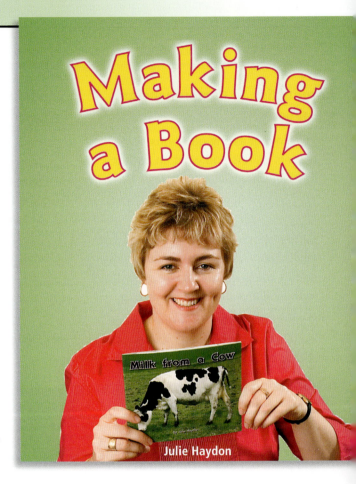

Book Talk
- Explain to children that as they read, they should ask questions to understand the author. Say *The author's name is Julie Haydon. Does that name sound familiar to you? She wrote many of the books we read in this program.*

- **Comprehension Strategy**
Explain to children that *brainstorm* means "to come up with lots of ideas quickly." Ask children to brainstorm some questions they have about how books are made. Record their questions on chart paper. Tell them that they will come back to this list after they have read *Making a Book.*

- Point out the table of contents. Ask *How many chapters does* Making a Book *have?* (eight)

Turn to page 2 — Book Talk

Revisiting the Text

Making a Book

Julie Haydon

Chapter 1	The Author	2
Chapter 2	What Kind of Book?	4
Chapter 3	The Idea	6
Chapter 4	Planning the Book	9
Chapter 5	The Words	12
Chapter 6	Putting the Book Together	14
Chapter 7	At the Printer	21
Chapter 8	The Readers	23
Glossary and Index		24

Future Vocabulary
- Have children look at the cover photograph. Point out that the author is holding a book. Show them that the books in your classroom are kept on a shelf. Ask *Where do you keep your books at home?* (on a shelf) *What else can you keep on a shelf?*

Now revisit pages 2–3

During Reading

Book Talk

- **Comprehension Strategy**
  What question does the author ask on page 3? (How is a book like this made?) Have children brainstorm ideas about how a book is made.

- Have children ask questions to better understand the author, such as *How did you learn to write books?* or *Why did you decide to write for children?*

- **Phonics Skill** Have children locate the word *children* on page 2. Ask *What letters does this word begin with? (ch)* Ask children to say /ch/ aloud together.

Turn to page 4 — Book Talk

Chapter 1 — The Author

My name is Julie Haydon.
I am an **author**.
I write books for children.

Revisiting the Text

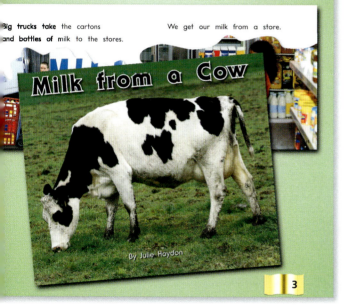

Future Vocabulary
- Point out the *shelf* of books that the author has over her desk on page 2. Ask *Why do you think she has so many books?* (Writers read a lot.) *What else does she have on a shelf?* (her computer, her computer monitor)

- **Comprehension Strategy** Tell children that a *pointed* question is a question that is to the point, or very direct, and aimed at a particular person or group. Ask *Were the questions you asked the author of* Making a Book *pointed questions?* (Yes, they were aimed at her.) *Give me an example of a pointed question you can ask the author after reading* Making a Book. (What other books have you written?)

Now revisit pages 4–5

3

During Reading

Book Talk
- Have children locate the word *publish* on page 4. Point out that *publish* is in dark, or boldfaced, type. Explain that this means the word is defined in the glossary at the back of the book.
- **Fluency Skill** Point out the commas on page 4. Explain that commas tell readers that they should take a short breath. Model reading page 4, taking short breaths at the appropriate places.
- Ask *What word on page 5 will we find in the glossary?* (nonfiction) *How do you know?* (It's in boldfaced type.) Have children turn to the glossary on page 24. Read aloud the definition of *nonfiction*.

Turn to page 6 — Book Talk

What Kind of Book?

First, the people who are going to make, or **publish**, my book tell me what they want.

Revisiting the Text

They want a **nonfiction** book on food.

The book must be sixteen pages long. It will have photographs in it.

5

Future Vocabulary
- Explain to children that *to point* means "to show where something is with your finger." For example, the woman on page 4 is using her finger to point to something on the table. Ask *What is the past tense of the word* point? *(pointed)* Ask a volunteer to create a sentence about this picture using the word *pointed*.

Now revisit pages 6–7

During Reading

Book Talk

- Have children locate the word *brainstorm* on page 6.
- Help children recall that the people who are going to publish the author's book want a nonfiction book about food. Say *Let's brainstorm some of our own ideas about a book about food.* Record their ideas on the board.
- Have a volunteer read aloud the author's list of ideas on page 7. Compare her ideas with the children's list of ideas.
- Ask *What are these colorful ovals with arrows?* (thought bubbles, thought balloons) *These are thought bubbles. They let us know what Julie is thinking about. What ideas is she thinking about here?* (cooking, cows and milk, what pets eat)

Turn to page 8 – Book Talk

Revisiting the Text

I write a list of ideas.
I do this on my computer.
The list looks like this:

Food ideas
- cooking
- a vegetable garden
- party food
- what pets eat
- cows and milk
- hens and eggs
- shopping for food

Future Vocabulary

- Say *The word* pointed *can also be used to describe something that has a sharp, narrow end. What on these pages has a* pointed *end?* (the thought bubbles, the author's pen)

Now revisit pages 8–9

During Reading

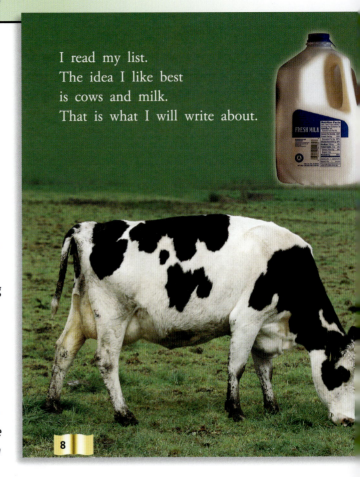

I read my list.
The idea I like best
is cows and milk.
That is what I will write about.

Book Talk

- **Comprehension Strategy**
  Explain to children that by asking questions of the author they are evaluating what they don't understand about what they're reading. This can also be a clue that the author should have given more information. Ask *What questions can you ask to help you understand the author better?* (Does it take a long time to come up with a writing plan? How will you find out about cows and milk?)

- Point out that Chapter 4 begins on page 9. Have a volunteer read the chapter title.

- **Fluency Skill** Say *A list like the one on page 9 is a text feature that gives us more information about what we are reading.* Read aloud the author's plan on page 9, modeling taking a breath at appropriate places.

Turn to page 10 – Book Talk

Revisiting the Text

Planning the Book

Chapter 4

I plan how I will write the book.

Cows and milk

We drink milk.
It is good for us.
Cows make milk.
Cows live on farms.
Farmers milk the cows.
The milk goes to a factory.
It is put into cartons and bottles.
These go to the stores.
We buy milk to drink.

Future Vocabulary
- Ask *Where do you keep milk at home?* (in the refrigerator) *Where do you put it in the refrigerator?* (on a shelf) *Where is milk kept at the store?* (on a shelf in the refrigerated section)

Now revisit pages 10–11

During Reading

Book Talk

- **Comprehension Strategy**
  Ask *Has the author answered any questions you have had? Which question?*

- **Phonics Skill** Have children locate the word *phone* on page 11. Have them say the word aloud. Ask *What consonants does* phone *begin with? (ph)*

➜ *Turn to page 12 — Book Talk*

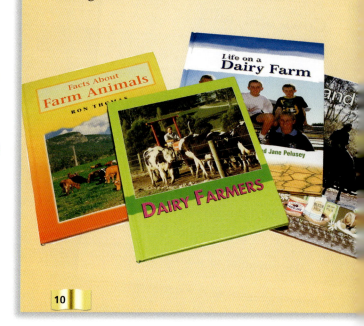

Revisiting the Text

I look up cows and milk on the **Internet**.

I talk on the phone to a farmer who has cows.

Future Vocabulary

- Point out the word *address* in the picture on page 11. Explain that the artwork is designed to look like a Web page from the Internet. Say *When you want to look up something on the Internet, you type in an address, which is a combination of letters, numbers, and other symbols. The address takes you to the Web site.* Explain that a Web site address is similar to a mailing address that people put on an envelope to send a letter.

Now revisit pages 12–13

During Reading

Book Talk

- Have children locate the word *publish* on these two pages. Ask *What does* publish *mean?* (make and print a book)

- **Comprehension Strategy** Ask *What question can you ask to understand the author now?* (What if the people who are going to publish your book do not like what you wrote? Are you finished with the book now?)

Turn to page 14 – Book Talk

Chapter 5

The Words

I write the words for the book on my computer.
It is hard work.

The words for the book look like this:

Milk from a Cow

Julie Haydon

Page 2
I like to drink milk.

Page 3
Where does milk come from?

Page 4
Milk comes from cows.
Cows live on farms.

Page 5
Cows eat grass, hay, and seeds.
Cows drink lots of water, too.

Page 6
The food and water help the cows to make the milk.

Page 7
[no text on this page, just a photo]

Page 8
It is time for the farmer to milk the cows.

Page 9
The cow go into a shed.

Page 10
A machine is in the shed.

Revisiting the Text

I send what I have written
to the people
who are going to publish my book.
I send my words by **e-mail**.

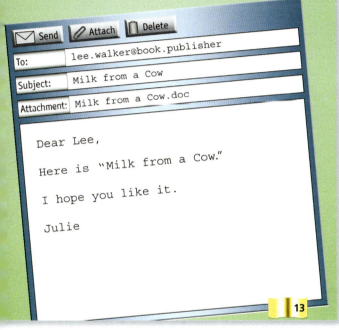

Future Vocabulary
- Explain that the artwork on page 13 is designed to look like an e-mail message. Point out the line that says *To.* Explain that on this line, the author has written the e-mail address of the editor. Like a Web site address, an e-mail address is a combination of words, letters, and other symbols. Ask *Do you or your parents have an e-mail address?*

Now revisit pages 14–15

During Reading

Book Talk

- Have children locate the word *editor*. Ask *Will this word be in the glossary?* (yes) *How do you know?* (It is in boldfaced type.) *Without looking at the glossary, can you tell me what an editor does?* (An editor checks the author's words for grammar and meaning.)

- Explain that the editor is one of the people who will help publish the author's book. Ask *Would you rather be an editor, a writer, or an illustrator for a book? Why?*

- Ask *Do you see a new text feature on this page?* (yellow highlighting) *The yellow highlighting shows how the editor changed the author's words.* Have children turn back to page 12 to compare manuscripts.

Turn to page 16 – Book Talk

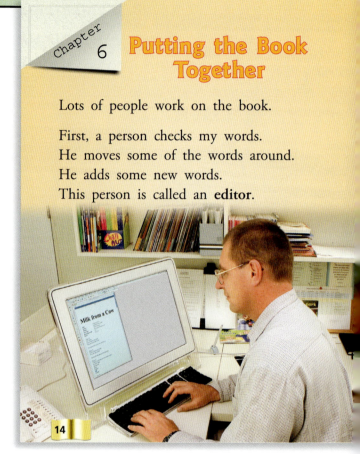

Chapter 6

Putting the Book Together

Lots of people work on the book.

First, a person checks my words.
He moves some of the words around.
He adds some new words.
This person is called an **editor**.

Revisiting the Text

Can you see what the editor has done? Turn back to page 12.

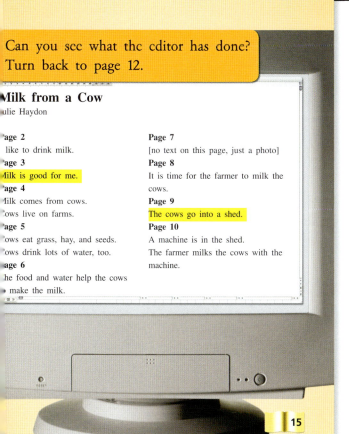

Milk from a Cow
Julie Haydon

Page 2
I like to drink milk.
Page 3
Milk is good for me.
Page 4
Milk comes from cows.
Cows live on farms.
Page 5
Cows eat grass, hay, and seeds.
Cows drink lots of water, too.
Page 6
The food and water help the cows to make the milk.

Page 7
[no text on this page, just a photo]
Page 8
It is time for the farmer to milk the cows.
Page 9
The cows go into a shed.
Page 10
A machine is in the shed.
The farmer milks the cows with the machine.

Future Vocabulary

- Point out to children that, like the author, the editor also has a shelf of books near his desk.

Now revisit pages 16–17

During Reading

Book Talk

- **Phonics Skill** Have children locate the words *photographs* and *photographer* on these pages. Have them say the words aloud. Ask *What consonants do these words begin with? (ph)*

- **Comprehension Strategy** Ask *What questions can you ask to understand the author better?* (Does the editor choose the photographs? Do you get to choose the photographs, too?)

Turn to page 18 – Book Talk

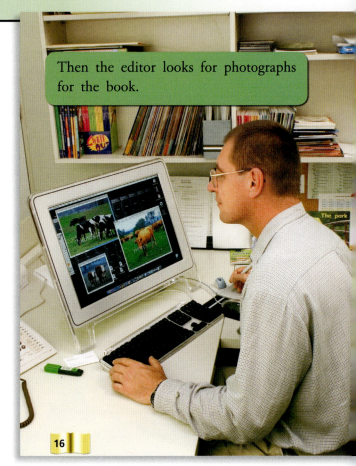

Then the editor looks for photographs for the book.

Revisiting the Text

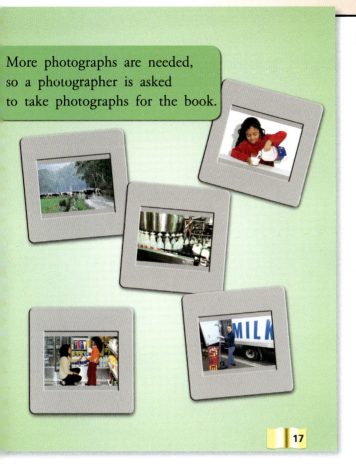

More photographs are needed, so a photographer is asked to take photographs for the book.

Future Vocabulary
- Explain that the plural form of *shelf* is *shelves*. Say *To make the word shelf plural, you change the f to a v and add -es. How many shelves does the editor have above his desk on page 16?* (two) *What does he keep on his shelves?* (books and papers)

Now revisit pages 18–19

During Reading

Book Talk

- **Phonics Skill** Have children locate the word *photographs* on page 18. Have children name other words that begin with *ph* such as *phrase*. (*phone, phantom, pharmacy, phase, phobia, phony, physical*) List the responses on the board.

- **Comprehension Strategy** Ask *After reading these pages, what questions can you ask to understand the author?* (Do all the people who help publish the book work on computers? Does the author help plan the book cover, too?)

Turn to page 20 – Book Talk

Next, a person puts the words and the photographs together. She does this on a computer. She plans the book cover, too.

Revisiting the Text

Future Vocabulary
- Explain that most Web site addresses begin with three *W*s that stand for World Wide Web. Most Web site addresses end with a period and the letters *com* for *commercial*, *edu* for *education*, or *org* for *organization*.
- Write on the board: *www._____.com* and have children use that form to make up an address for a Web site about cows and milk.

Now revisit pages 20–21

During Reading

Book Talk
- Have children locate the word *editor* on these pages.
- Point out the *editor* may make changes to the sample pages. There may be mistakes in the words, or the *editor* may want to change the words. Explain that the *editor* often uses red pencil to make these changes. Ask *Why do you think the editor uses red pencils?* (so the markings will stand out)

Turn to page 22 – Book Talk

Revisiting the Text

At the Printer

Chapter 7

The book is ready to be printed.
Big machines at the printer
print each book on a big sheet of paper.

Each sheet of paper is folded
and cut into pages.
The book covers and pages are stapled together.

Future Vocabulary
- Explain to children that when the editor made changes to the sample book pages, he pointed out some mistakes in the words. Have children recall what color the editor used when he pointed out these mistakes. (red)
- Challenge children to find a shelf on these pages. (behind the printing presses)

Now revisit pages 22–23

During Reading

Book Talk
- Leave this page spread for children to discover on their own when they read the book individually.

Turn to page 24 – Book Talk

The book is published! The book goes to bookstores, schools, and libraries. I get a box of books, too.

Revisiting the Text

The Readers

Children read my book. They talk about cows and milk with their teacher.

Chapter 8

Future Vocabulary
- Explain that the publisher sent the books to the author. Ask *How did the mail carrier know where to leave the box of books?* (The publisher put the author's *address* on the box.)
- Tell children that *address* can also mean "to speak to a group." Ask *Who is addressing the group of children on page 23?* (a teacher, a librarian)

Go to page T5 – Revisiting the Text

During Reading

Book Talk

* Note: Point out this text feature page as a reference point for children's usage while reading independently.

Individual Reading

Have each child read the entire book at his or her own pace while remaining in the group.

Go to page T5 – Revisiting the Text

Glossary

author	a person who writes books and stories
brainstorm	to come up with lots of ideas quickly
editor	a person who checks the words and photos in a book
e-mail	mail sent by computer
Internet	lots of computers that are linked together and share information
nonfiction	a story about facts, not a made-up story
publish	to make and print a book
sample	something that shows what a finished thing will look like

Index

brainstorm 6
cover 18, 21
editor 14, 15, 16, 20
e-mail 13
idea 6, 7, 8
Internet 11

library 10, 22
nonfiction 5
photographer 17
photos 5, 16, 17, 18
publish 4, 13, 22
sample pages 19, 20

24

During independent work time, children can read the online book at:
www.rigbyflyingcolors.com

Revisiting the Text

Future Vocabulary
- Use the notes on the right-hand pages to develop oral vocabulary that goes beyond the text. These vocabulary words first appear in future texts. These words are: *shelf*, *address*, and *pointed*.

  Turn back to page 1

Reading Vocabulary Review
Activity Sheet: Word Sorter
- Write the word *brainstorm* on the board and divide it into its two parts. (*brain* and *storm*)
- Have children write *brainstorm* on the top line of the Word Sorter and *brain* and *storm* on the second line. Have children complete the chart with descriptions of the two smaller words.

Comprehension Strategy Review
Use Interactive Modeling Card: Nonfiction Questions and Answers
- Review some of the questions children asked during the lesson. Then discuss things children learned while reading.
- Use this discussion to complete the Nonfiction Questions and Answers chart.

Phonics Review
- Have children look for words that begin with the consonant digraphs *ch* and *ph*. (*chapter:* pp. 1, 2, 4, 6, 9, 12, 14, 21, 23; *children:* pp. 2, 23; *checks:* p. 14; *photographs:* pp. 5, 16–18; *photographer:* p. 17; *phone:* p. 11)
- Have children brainstorm other words that begin with *ch* and *ph*. Make a list of responses for each digraph. Have children pick a word from each list and write a sentence using each word they picked.

Fluency Review
- Turn to page 6. Partner children and have them take turns reading this page to each other.
- Tell them to take breaths at appropriate times, such as when they see a comma or a period.

Reading-Writing Connection
Activity Sheet: Main Idea and Supporting Details

To assist children with linking reading and writing:
- Have children complete the Main Idea and Supporting Details chart for *Making a Book*.
- Then have children use the completed Activity Sheet to plan and write their own book.

4 Assessment

Assessing Future Vocabulary

Work with each child individually. Ask questions that elicit each child's understanding of the Future Vocabulary words. Note each child's responses:

- What do you store on a shelf at home?
- Do you know where someone lives if all you know is his or her e-mail address?
- If something has a pointed end, is it sharp or dull?

Assessing Comprehension Strategy

Work with each child individually. Note each child's understanding of asking questions to understand an author:

- How does asking questions help you better understand what you're reading?
- What types of questions can you ask the author? Give some examples.
- Was each child able to explain why asking the author questions can help a reader understand the text?

Assessing Phonics

Work with each child individually. Show each child word cards of *ch* and *ph* words. Have each child read the words aloud and point to the consonant digraph. Note each child's responses for understanding of the consonant digraphs *ch* and *ph*:

- Use the following words: *children, check, chapter, phone, photograph,* and *photographer.*
- Did each child understand the sound that the letters *ch* make?
- Did each child understand that the letters *ph* sound like the letter *f*?

Assessing Fluency

Have each child read page 18 to you. Note each child's understanding of taking a breath at appropriate times:

- Did each child take a short breath at commas?
- Did each child take a longer breath at the end of sentences?
- Was each child able to decode the word *photograph,* which has the *ph* digraph?

Interactive Modeling Cards

Word Log

Title: *Making a Book*

Word	Meaning from Selection
shelf	place for storing things
address	location (Web site, e-mail, or postal address); speak to
pointed	direct; past tense of point; sharp end

Directions: With children, fill in the Word Log using the words *shelf*, *address*, and *pointed*.

Nonfiction Questions and Answers

Before Reading		During Reading	After Reading
What do I know about this topic?	What do I want to find out by reading this book?	What did I learn?	What new questions do I have?
Authors write books.	How do authors come up with ideas?	Some authors write just for children.	How do you learn to be an author?
Books can be about true things or made-up things.	How much do authors get paid to write a book?	Authors do not work alone.	Is it hard to write books?

Directions: With children, fill in the Nonfiction Questions and Answers chart for *Making a Book*.

Discussion Questions

- What kinds of books does this author write? (Literal)
- Did the author do a good job of explaining how a book is made? (Critical Thinking)
- Do you think the author enjoys her job? (Inferential)

Activity Sheets

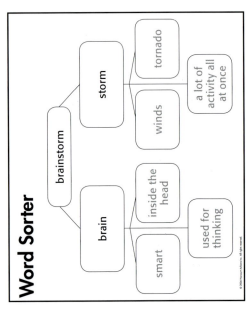

Directions: Have children fill in the Word Sorter using the word *brainstorm*.

Directions: Have children fill in the Main Idea and Supporting Details for *Making a Book*.
Optional: Have children use another copy of the Activity Sheet to plan and write their own short book.